Lucy's Bone Scrolls:
The Black Speculative Mystery School

Sherese Francis

Three-Legged Elephant Publishing
New York

Copyright © 2017 by Sherese Francis

All rights reserved.
No part of this publication may be reproduced, distributed, or transmitted in any form or by any means, including photocopying, recording, or other electronic or mechanical methods, without the prior written permission of the publisher, except in the case of brief quotations embodied in critical reviews and certain other noncommercial uses permitted by copyright law.

Design and Formatting by Sherese Francis
Manufactured in the United States of America

Book Cover Picture: Cropped image of original Louis Armstrong Playing Trumpet for His Wife, Lucille, in Front of the Sphinx by the Pyramids in Giza, 1961. Credit by Associated Press
Author picture credit: Rosalyn Fernandez

*for everyone who has supported and inspired me
and yes I'm talking about you!*

Table of Contents

Narrative Technology	*9*
The Narrative Technology (Part II)	*11*
A State of Being:	*12*
The Image of God as The Cowardly Lion (How to Act Despite My Fears)	*13*
The Scientific Method (The Theory of Consciousness' Cycle)	*14*
TechnoGriot Spotlight	*17*
(I)Magine (The Fugitive Imaginings of a Black Spring Goddess)	*19*
What Is Black Love?	*21*
I Am What I Will Be (or I Will Be What I Am)	*23*
The Constant State of Imagination (Rage)	*24*
Black Girl Magik with Harriet's Apothecary	*25*
The Legend of the Masked Fencer (I Can't Help But Wander)	*26*
Forbidden Fruit (Love is Strange)	*30*
Beloved	*35*
41 Cents & A Dream	*37*
Shame of America	*38*
What Ifs	*40*
Shadow Puppetry/ Cosmic Quilt	*42*

Congregation of Blues Print:
                                                                    Esthetic

Revolutionary Design
                                                  Ecstatic

I.
Narrative Technology

Our stories be
                survival tools &
               healing medicine
             moving us
               raising us up
Our stories be mutinies
pirate spaceships
stealing back legacies — ark of the arkive
                      ark of bones
                      ark of the nu
          break/through
the technoveil
             of white reality:
fiction of race
        pushed against
          piercing through
like bullets into
              our skins.
Will future   force the meaning
          of skin to change shape?
What would an/other world look like
if the world didn't
        exist
        as we know it now?
What would Octavia do?

II.
Goals

Explore technology's dark side;
dark matter wefting between spaces of creation.
Crystal ball tellers of originality:
Get dirty———-—> Get mixed <———— Get wet
      We   creation on a potter's wheel planet
                divine reflection made of clay.
God/She must of had a dirty mind —
liked the feel of Her fingers coiling life into shape.
III.
Is future moving forward?
Maybe it moves in re/verse
like newborn to ancient ancestor to newborn again?
Like revolution will begin again?
Like imagination bending body
                back to the time is now
coming back around to knock you out.
What do you see in your crystal ball constellation?
Wicked witch? Or Narcissus in the image pool?
Rippling reflection?:
We be both mad scientists & monsters.
We be both science & fiction.
We keep fighting this world to create an/other:
sailing to touch the dark mind of the cosmos; to see
ourselves in its identification card &
be given permission to live.

The Narrative Technology (Part II) -- Expansion of Perception

Surgeon General Report:
Too much consumption
can ruin your appetite
for creating
new languages --
Be hungry like the muni bird!

How do we recreate the pyramids?
How do we make tombs
                        into portals
                        to the other
worlds again?

What wisdoms of the world;
what possibilities have we lost
in our mad dash to prove our progress? to leave
the ancient behind
even as it courses through our veins
& shows up in our face?

Where have we been & to
where are we moving:
what is the dia(gnosis) of our art.

A State of Being:
woman questioning sameness
black woman demoted from divine
sphinx in human form
stardust remolded into life
galaxy of stars crafting spirals
uni/verse projected
possibility of multi/verses
roots of compounds & breakdowns
mouth & eye of most high
silent thought of creation
manifestations of a cosmic body
: Chimerical reaction

The Image of God as The Cowardly Lion (How to Act Despite My Fears)

Finding a way to move on
is the endless procession
of a missionary preaching
survival: how to outlive

the hollows of wounds —
dance like needles within
wounds   dance around
wounds   dress wounds
like egungun like sensay
like costume character
like mummy medicine   divine
despite your feet
trembling at each step.
Make it a dance. Make it shake the earth.
Make the rocks cry out with your steps.

Find a way to speak magic
even when you know your image will be sold &
will be sacrificed on the world's pole.
Always be ready to dance once again,
easing down the road into resurrection.

The Scientific Method (The Theory of Consciousness' Cycle)

"The mind which has conceived a plan of living must never lose sight of the chaos against which that pattern was conceived" - Ralph Ellison

Purpose- What do you want to learn?
How are Manifest Destiny, building a house & industrial society alike?

Research- Find out as much as you can.
Jesus told Peter the church would be built on the rock.
Peter means rock. Peter — the same man who rejected Jesus three times.
Peter — the root of petrification: the wild wood turned to stone. The living matter replaced with minerals to preserve structure.
To turn to stone out of fear. To turn to stone to remember.
Medusa turned men who feared her into stone. Looking at the wild mother did not turn them into stone, fear of her did.
The foundation of civilization is stone, is fear. The fear of the wild mother turns you into stone. A prophecy full of itself:
The Monument.. The Obelisk. The Djed. The Statue. The Pyramid. The Shrine of a Muse.

The Status. The Institution. The Industry. The Secret Society.
The Fixed Image. The Building. The Museum.
The Dead Image. The Tomb. The Gravestone. The Mausoleum.
The Reminder. The Memory. The Skeleton. The Body of Lot's Wife. The Hoodoo Rock.
The Extension Beyond the Living Self. The Art. The Technology. The Resurrection.
The Tin Man's Gospel.

Hypothesis- Try to predict the answer to the problem. Another term for hypothesis is 'educated guess'. This is usually stated like " If I...(do something) then...(this will occur).
If We learn. We remember. We create. We build.

Against fear. Against insecurity. Against the outside. Against the other. Against the wild. Against the dark. Against the wounding. Against the void.

Then We all want eternal life. We all fear death. We all want safety. We all avoid.

Experiment- Design a test or procedure to confirm or disprove your hypothesis. Design it in a reproducible manner.
Why am I writing this?
Experience tells me

that I fear my own Mind
will eat me alive if I do not let it
express itself into form.
My Mind fears forgetting.
My Mind fears being forgotten.
My Mind fears it will not understand
Itself and You.

Analysis- Record what happened during the experiment. Also known as 'data'.
This poem is my record.
Is remembered by my heart.
I spread it everywhere so there are no outsiders.
I have decorated my cage
against the variable chaos
looming outside
the white picket fence.

Conclusion- Review the data. Check to see if your hypothesis was correct.
History repeats because we do not bother to
investigate ourselves.
Do not learn the roots of our own actions.
Do not answer our own primal question.
This is not a linear process but instead is a constant
cycle of inquiry:
for this Self continues to forget
I will do it again.

TechnoGriot Spotlight

Cultivating evangelist:
flying messenger
carrying a nation of images,
dispersing reflections,
scattering of exiled
seeds dying to live again —
shapeshifters in new environments:

      ancients passed down
in new apps,
the tech of story
scrying on the screen of chaos,
passing through technoveil,
the flash of spirit when plugging into the cave:

We   greedy for fruits
& carrying home on our backs We
      search for elders' magic drums
like data thieves We   steal back our legacies
We   shape spirit twins of our souls We
form ourselves again in the dark room
of space & find the right exposure
for our dark faces We
      recreate wounds into nu brands, nu senses:

this is the re-evolution of the camera.
The alien image finding new ways to capture itself

into the dark ground & find light inside earth,
find nu (or is it old) blueprints in its foundation
& repeat them like spells.
Those ancient patterns woven into skin
the vision originally created: We reshaped from
Mind — skin inscribed with divine ink of light.

(I)Magine (The Fugitive Imaginings of a Black Spring Goddess)

She imagined a world where she could breathe
Her body was enough to stop bullets
She had powers to make her visions realities
She would see the world through the eye of space
See the universe in its entirety not just Herself
See She was the universe; space & time too
She could throw a dart at injustice
& make it disappear with love
like the charge in Cupid's arrow
She could feel
everyone's story flow
through her body
& she would die
& be born again each time
She would let them whisper to her
She would let them use her voice
because she owed that to them
But She would use her voice for Herself first
She would consume her rage
before anyone else could
She would call out those who abandoned her
She would sew up her wounds like a quilt
Her scars a secret code of a map, a constellation of futures
She would search for futures
outside of cages

outside of auction block stages
outside of greedy watchful eyes
like waves in a particle-wave theory
She imagined she was the waves
She was the ocean
She was the Earth
She was creator & creation
She was the Dark Universe
full of stars
She saw Herself
whole again.

What is Black Love?

God in an infinite sense.
God in a plural tense.
Time stretched beyond
known beginnings & ends.
Love: a strengthening of muscles
of the heart to hold
the many loves
the many voices
the many gods
into one body of beauty.

Love: the boundless horizon.
The continuous expansion of the mind.
The universal fragmentation &
single ship connection
relation ship connection
friend ship connection.
The exploration of gray matter &
revealer of the skin's mask.
The question & the quest.
The courage to leave, to die, to grow &
the courage to stay.
The embrace of spirit & earth
like the way clouds love a mountain:
not as possession but as finding freedom
in knowing each other exist, are still here.
Knowing yours & another's space.

This state of grace
in being
together.

I Am What I Will Be (or I Will Be What I Am)

What would I be
if I wasn't told what I am;
if I wasn't classified?
Would I be sun?
Would I be earth?
Would I be rain?
Would I be wind?
Would I be new growth
of the universe's imagination?
Would I be able to stretch
into the far reaches of dreams?
Beyond the cages of this world?
Beyond illusions into
possibilities of dark body?
into spiral dances of dark body?
into creative flow of dark body?
Would I realize I am what I am?

The Constant State of Imagination (Rage)

Dia(gnosis): Rage

The Righteous Anger! The This Is Why You Mad! The Madness! The Mad Scientist! The Bandit of Birthright! The Audacity! The Fierceness! The Fiery Passion! The Furies! The You Don't Quite Fit! The You're Too Black! The You're Not Black Enough! The You Too Much! The My Cup Overfloweth! The Marginal! The Variable! The Peripheral Vision! The Hallucinator! The Revelator! The Dreamer! The Poet Prophet! The Ecstatic Spirit! The Holy Ghost Worshipper! The God Whisperer! The Manic Mantic! The Out of One's Mind! The Dance Battler Forcing Movement! The Wanderer! The Migrant! The Exiled! The Refugee! The Reject! The Mocker! The Jester! The Irrational Storm! The Blown Fuse! The Circuit Breaker! The Decoder! The Ego Tripper! The Fugitive Slave! The Drapetomaniac! The Escapologist! The Robin Hood of Columbusing Thievery! Yes! That Mother/Fucker!
Dancing! Dancing! Dancing!
Revolution!

Black Girl Magik with Harriet's Apothecary

What is the meaning of our names?
Did you know Harriet was a spy?
Did you know she changed her name to her
mother's?
Hid in her name. Fled in her name. Found freedom
in her name. What will I find in her name?
Lineage of first name stretching over body
& survival beyond the (k)now   beyond
     the ledge
the wounds are the same
medicine of dreams, medicine that manifest
dreams into being. Medicine women please help me
remember:
My body!+My mind!+My (e)motions!+My
spirit!+My others!+Others' me!+All the me's!——
—>
Moving beyond reaction
to the state of being
One.
Peace.

The Legend of The Masked Fencer (I Can't Help But Wander)

Have you ever thought
     about what's beyond
     my dark mask?
Have you ever desired
     my true face?
Have you only seen
     my swords as threat,
    a trinity of varied gravities?
Each move I make you've perceived
as attack
     not as a dance
     not as a struggle to crack open
the shell of old worlds.
These swords
     like musical bows,
     like charged arrows of sound,
are filled with lightning;
they make cuts
into hearts
     like striking a tree.
I heard you
    only can grow
when you are broken.

These swords
     like needles

with which I warp
                worlds together,
surviving   tripping
on the spinning of stories
& with the waves of my hands
they magically appear.
I juggle multiplicities of me
both   afraid & hopeful
you will see
              past my sleights of hand.
Higher powers label me a contagion
but I build their illusions of immunity.
I am a carpenter of inner and outer workings.
I inject myself first. I break my own skin daily.

These swords are boring tools —
              I bury seeds.
              I dig up treasure.
              I find a place to go
when the sun no longer shines;
tunneling my way through
to the other side &
              planting myself in the dark
like entering the innermost temple:
a storehouse of forgotten names of gods.
              I give them new
bodies to live in.
These swords I bundle together,
making a gate around my body &

leaving part of it loose to be opened.
       I've been waiting to
welcome you in.
These swords like pens write me
on the inner walls of home;
sometimes I imagine they are feathers
       & together they are
wings to fly away.

These swords are my fight to be free,
    my fight to love,
    my fight to defend
what I hold dear.
Sometimes I protect myself from love.
Sometimes I protect love from me.
Sometimes I cloak myself in a straight-jacket
   armor of white
    encasing my darkness
wrapping piercing thoughts of my mind
between two battle snakes
for our protection.
Or maybe they painted me like this
for their own.
It's been so long,
I barely remember;
but I know about playing the game;
I have not deceived myself.
       I know who I am
underneath.

I have learned to live
with not being seen
& I wait for those who wander beyond
                                      my dark face.

Forbidden Fruit (Love Is Strange)

This is not a fairytale's
happy ever after.
This is a court record
of my testimony
& my sentencing:

the conviction of the guilty
for taking a beauty which by man's law
I was told I couldn't have,
like I stole fire from a heaven
we didn't deserve.
I am delivered up
by a betrayer's kiss that chose me,
pinned me like to a cross, blessed me in blood &
branded me with a red beastly mark

into my chest for submitting to my desire,
for satisfying my curiosity.
For being like Eve, who wanted to be like God
& pluck songs
off of freedom's tangled web that now hangs me —

by these words may I be born again &
attract the hungry fire of belly
that pierces fruit rinds
& finds new discovery
in something I have folded into myself:

hiding in the flaming skin
of dragon fruit
in the monstrous fingers
of buddha's hands
in the horned fish kiwano
in the flowering massive jackfruit body
in the messy bed hair of rambutan
in the bulging eyes & twisted shape
of magnolia —
the greatest beauty found within
a frightening face is what

I give to a stranger to reveal myself.
A stranger who will want
to drink my filling juices,
who has eyes to see me as go(o)d;
see that I have paid the price of entry;
see that I wanted dirt, I wanted the ground
to open up & dance with all of its faults & mine;
eat my shell, the rain & the sun
whole & raise hell like a
rocket ship, elevating my breaking bark
into a howl.

*Art of Black: Where Past & Future Become One;
From Where Magic Is Birthed*

Beloved

Love for us is a quiet collision.
A conspiracy: we
breathe together;
a revolution against a current state
of being:

We

blend boundaries of becoming.
Float on each other's air
like the interference of sound waves,
like a fish's organ evolved for buoyancy,
like the intersection of all the places we meet.
We be atoms of your body
reacting with mine:

We

have been broken
& reordered
to be
bodies nu:
ourselves
formed in the shape
of home.
A bond so unbreakable
that we exist as one another

& there is no point that exists
where you & I end.

Can you see
your face in me?
The face of another
possible?

41 Cents & A Dream

How much of a dream
could I buy with just the change
left in my pocket?

If this altar is
its resting place along with
my blood & broken

reflection, is it
enough for the collection
plate? Does the emptied

shells I offer: my
dark mask, scraps of hearts & friends
be enough to buy

a dream to outlive
me, wash me clean, not let a
future erase me?

Shame of America
in memory of Laura Nelson and other victims of lynchings

A rocking chair
                Find mama inside
Fall asleep
                In her chest
Neck breaking
                Noose
Let me kiss
                The marks on your neck
Hanging man
                Stand your ground
See the world
                Upside down
Iron bit
                Drowning tongue
Suckling metal
                I want milk
Her breasts
                For me?
I can't rest head
                March
See the bridge
                Body pushed out of a moving
When is the train coming?
                A Woman was
Lynched today

```
                        I see her
In the water
                        Swaying with wind
Her name
                        Mama
Mama
            Mama
Her name
                        Me
Me
            Me
What happened to my baby?
```

What Ifs

I can't help but think

Of what ifs

Of remembering distant memories

Of visions from another space

Of reaching my black hand across oceans

Of reaching past the sun

Of singing codes

Of body switching

Of my family taken instead

Of my family staying where we were

Of plantation by another name

Of plantation by another time

Of revolutions & machetes

Of fugitivity & migration

Of the sanctuary of trees

Of growing with master's farm tools

Of ancestors in masks hovering behind

Of conjuring memories in costume

Of ritual & possession

Of what it would be like to be another

Of names I never knew I could be

Of you become me & I become you

Of histories finding themselves at my door

like long lost cousins

& finding out we both

have the same shoe size.

Shadow Puppetry

My shadow contained
the universe in its self
& I bowed to it

Cosmic Quilt

Portals opened: eyes
deciphering patterns in
stitches of fabric

cross culture spiral —
spirit's twisting code: I am
in tune with design.

Notes

Section I of the chapbook was based on the first Afrofuturism conference at the New School in 2015.

Section II was based on the Black Magic: Afro Pasts/Futures exhibition at the Brooklyn Corridor Gallery in 2016. Below are the artworks that inspired each piece:

"Beloved" was inspired by Arnold Butler's "Mutual Feelings and "Duality."

"41 Cents & A Dream" was inspired by Soraya Jean Louis McElroy's work of the same name.

"Shame of America" was inspired by Soraya Jean Louis McElroy's work of the same name.

"What Ifs" was inspired by Delphine Fawundu's "Mende Woman on Nat Turner Plantation," "She Remembers the Turner Plantation and "Mende Woman Sees the Turner Plantation" from the Deconstructing She series.

"Shadow Puppetry" was inspired DJ Underdog's slideshow and "Cosmic Quilt" was inspired by Charles Jean Pierre's "Invisible Barriers" and "Cultural DNA."

Acknowledgements

Thank you to Malcolm Boyd of Three-Legged Elephant Publishing for giving me the motivation to publish my first chapbook.

Thank you to my writing communities, J.P. Howard and Women Writers in Bloom, and Dave Johnson and Free Verse (Yasmine, Nicole, Lala, George, Napoleon, Yoelin) for helping me to grow as a writer.

Thank you to my mother and father for providing support for me as I pursue my writing career.

Finally, thank you to the 2015 Afrofuturism Conference at The New School and *Black Magic: Afro Pasts/Futures* exhibition curated by Niama Safia Sandy for giving me the material to produce the poems in this book.

Biography

Sherese Francis is a southeast Queens-based published poet, writer, blogger and literary curator. She has published work in journals and anthologies like Newtown Literary, Blackberry Magazine, Kalyani Magazine, African Voices, *Near Kin: A Collection of Words and Arts Inspired by Octavia Butler* and *Bared: Contemporary Poetry and Art on Bras and Breasts*. Her current projects include her Afrofuturism-inspired blog, Futuristically Ancient; and her southeast Queens-based pop up bookshop/mobile library, *J. Expressions*, which is dedicated to promoting and growing the literary community in the area, and for which she received a 2017 Queens Council on the Arts grant.

Made in the USA
Columbia, SC
14 August 2021